IS THE BIBLE RELIABLE?

building the historical case

LESSON 1

THE PATRIARCHAL NARRATIVES AND THE DOCUMENTARY HYPOTHESIS

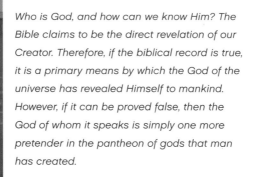

Who is God, and how can we know Him? The Bible claims to be the direct revelation of our Creator. Therefore, if the biblical record is true, it is a primary means by which the God of the universe has revealed Himself to mankind. However, if it can be proved false, then the God of whom it speaks is simply one more pretender in the pantheon of gods that man has created.

In this introductory lesson, Dr. Stephen Meyer begins to lay a historical foundation for the accuracy of the biblical text by looking into the lives of the early Patriarchs, namely Abraham and his descendants. In so doing, he starts to build the case for the historicity of Scripture. Is the Bible true? You decide.

QUOTE UNQUOTE

What did Dr. Meyer say? Fill in the blanks as you watch his presentation..

1. The Bible is arguably the _____ book in human history that claims to be the revelation of the same God who made the universe.

2. The heart cannot exult in what the _____ _____.

3. With a theistic worldview, you can at least be open to the possibility of _____.

4. _____ evidence corroborates the testimony of the patriarchal narratives, both directly and indirectly.

5. Several classes of external archaeological evidence have shown that the _____ _____ is untenable.

6. The biblical text contains _____ _____ that could not have been known long after the fact.

7. Naturalistic assumptions about the origin of the Bible give rise to a view of the Bible that is at odds with the _____ and _____ evidence.

8. The use of _____ names for God in the Torah does not establish the existence of _____ authors or sources.

9. The external evidence _____ the origin of the biblical text close to the time of the events it describes.

10. "The grass withers, the flower fades, but the _____ ___ _____ _____ stands forever" (Isaiah 40:8).

WHAT'S THE BIG IDEA?

THE BIBLE CAN'T BE FACT IF GOD IS FICTION.

DISBELIEF IN THE EXISTENCE OF GOD

leads people to doubt the historical accuracy of the Bible, since it makes sense only if its account of God's intervention in history is true.

Four Score and seven years ago, our fathers brought forth on this continent, a new nation, conceived in Liberty, and dedicated to the proposition that all men are created equal . . .

Obviously at least four different people composed this speech . . .

The Mathematician, (four score and seven), The Libertarian, (conceived in Liberty), the Logician, (proposition), and the Male Chauvinist (all men).

HAVE FAITH IN ABRAHAM

AN IMPRESSIVE AMOUNT of archaeological and other documentary evidence shows that the stories of Abraham, Isaac, and Jacob must have originated close to the time of the events they describe and are therefore historically reliable.

SINCE THE BIBLE'S ACCOUNT of key historical events seems to be accurate, then what it says about God's acting in those events is likely to be accurate as well.

I've got an assignment for you Abram. The human race needs to be rescued!

Yes, Lord, but what's that got to do with me?

It's a long story that starts with you.

Do you really need me? Can't you do it yourself?

Trust me, Abe, before it's over I'll be more involved than you ever imagined.

Discuss as a group what you would say if your teacher or professor asked the following question in class:

What sort of evidence makes you think the biblical stories of Abraham, Isaac, and Jacob are historical fact?

Support or add to one another's responses, bringing in any relevant Bible passages. Perhaps you'd like to role-play the dialogue, taking turns to represent the skeptical professor.

Blowing in the Wind

In the late 1800s, Julius Wellhausen and other scholars began to think that religion had just evolved over time. According to this theory, mankind had moved naturally—without any divine revelation—from pantheism or animism ("god" in nature) to polytheism (many "gods") to monotheism (one God, outside of nature). This evolutionary view came on the heels of Charles Darwin's On the Origin of Species *(1859), which set out his theory of biological evolution. A coincidence? Or could this be what the apostle Paul meant when he said that people are "tossed to and fro by the waves and carried about by every wind of doctrine, by human cunning" (Ephesians 4:14, ESV)?*

Another Duh Moment

"A professor of theology has the practical task of preparing the students for service in the Protestant church, ... but instead ... I make my hearers unfit for their office."

Julius Wellhausen
on resigning from his professorship

WHAT IS WHAT?

Draw a line from each term in the first column to its definition in the second column.

PRIME REALITY

- many authors wrote the first five books of the Bible

HIGHER CRITICISM

- the world was created by a Supreme Being

DOCUMENTARY HYPOTHESIS

- biblical narratives have no historical basis

MIRACLE

- researching the author/source and purpose of biblical texts

PATRIARCHAL

- when something doesn't seem to belong to the time period it has been assigned to

THEISTIC WORLDVIEW

- the period of Israel's history dominated by Abraham, Isaac, Jacob, and Joseph

SITUATES

- Old Testament stories, though loosely based on real people or events, are mostly fiction

ANACHRONISM

- when a story's details help pinpoint its actual historical setting

BIBLICAL NIHILISM

- the source of everything else (Exodus 3:14 "I am who I am")

BIBLICAL MINIMALISM

- an act of God; something not explainable by natural laws

LESSON 2

THE EXODUS: FROM EGYPT TO CANAAN

The Exodus story is one of the longest continuous narratives in the entire Bible, and it has significant historical and theological implications for both Christians and non-Christians. The story starts with Joseph's being sold into slavery in Egypt and imprisoned, then rising to prominence under Pharaoh and saving his family from a great famine. Once Joseph dies, his descendants (the Israelites) are forced into bondage by the Egyptians. After four hundred years, the Lord rescues them by having Moses lead them out of Egypt, across the Red Sea, and into the wilderness to wander for another 40 years before conquering the Promised Land. It is a tale of epic proportions, but did it really happen? Can we prove that the Israelites were even in Egypt, or that they later escaped Pharaoh's grasp and fled into the desert?

Historians have discussed this narrative for centuries, wondering how such incredible events could have taken place. But this is more than just a great drama; the Exodus is a revealing look into the nature and character of God Himself. He is portrayed as the author and writer of history. He brings forth justice on the unjust and mercy for the persecuted. He remembers and rescues His people. He is the author of salvation, and it is He who controls the destiny of mankind.

QUOTE UNQUOTE

What did Dr. Meyer say? Fill in the blanks as you watch his presentation..

1. If you hold a materialistic worldview, then the _____
   ___ _____ _____ _____ simply cannot have occurred.

2. The typical defenses of the historical reliability of the Bible
   have been essentially arguments from _____.

3. There is a lot of extra-biblical evidence that the Egyptians
   had large public building projects involving the forced labor
   of _____ slaves.

4. From the time of King David right up to the Babylonian
   conquest, the most common style of Israelite architecture
   was the _____ house.

5. We find distinctive Hebrew names in the _____
   _____ of Egyptian households. Were the Israelites
   present in Egypt? It certainly appears that they were.

5. The Amarna letters refer to raids and conquest of several
   Canaanite cities by a group of _____.

6. Why are the _____ talking about the Israelites
   in 1400 B.C.?

7. An archaeological inscription mentioning "_____ _____
   _____" by itself puts to rest the whole school of
   biblical minimalism on the question of the Exodus.

8. There was a migration of Israelites from Egypt to Canaan
   about the middle of the 15th century B.C., otherwise known
   as the _____.

WHAT'S THE BIG IDEA?

A PYRAMID SCENE

WE KNOW FROM ARCHAEOLOGICAL

evidence that the Israelites were slaves in Egypt before 1446 B.C., just as the Bible says.

Let's use the same architecture when we get to the Promised Land.

Sorta like leaving a bread crumb trail?

You got it!

Clever!

WHAT'S THE BIG IDEA?

THEY MADE IT TO CANAAN (FINALLY)

WE KNOW FROM ARCHAEOLOGICAL

evidence that the Israelites arrived in the land of Canaan around 1400 B.C., just as the Bible claims.

FOOTPRINTS IN THE SAND

WE HAVE ARCHAEOLOGICAL EVIDENCE

of the Israelites wandering in the wilderness between Egypt and Canaan, just as the Bible says.

Discuss as a group what you would say if your teacher or professor asked the following question in class:

What specific evidence is there to support the Bible's claim that the Israelites once lived in Egypt and then made their way to Canaan around 1400 B.C.?

You can refer to your notes, if you took any during Dr. Meyer's lecture. For each piece of evidence, tell the group what the document or artifact is called and what it reveals. (If possible, include where it was discovered.) Support or add to one another's responses so that the group can come up with a long list of evidence. Perhaps you'd like to role-play the dialogue, taking turns to represent the skeptical professor.

Be Your Own Archaeologist

The crossing of the Red Sea. Mt. Sinai. The Ark of the Covenant. Who wouldn't want to don Indiana Jones's fedora and go searching for the actual biblical locations and artifacts? Many archaeologists and amateurs have done so with mixed results.

Enough evidence has been uncovered to throw into doubt the traditional location of the sea crossing and Mt. Sinai. But the evidence is not definitive, and further research is complicated by governments who keep explorers at a distance.

Nothing can stop the Internet adventurer who embarks on a search for the facts. You may want to start with the Base Institute (baseinstitute.org). Whatever you find, remember that the evidence unearthed in this lecture is every bit as fascinating and more reliable in providing extra-biblical proof of Scripture's accuracy.

WHAT IS WHAT?

Draw a line from each term in the first column to its definition in the second column.

1446 B.C.

• ancient Egyptian reference to various people groups living in Canaan

ARGUMENT FROM SILENCE

• nomadic, marauding tribes in the Middle East—possibly referring to the Israelites themselves

ASIATICS

• detailed match between the biblical and archaeological records

430 YEARS

• inscription that proves the Israelites were a dominant group in Canaan by around 1209 B.C.

SPECIFICITY

• area of ancient Palestine west of the Jordan River, the Promised Land of the Israelites

HABIRU

• when the Exodus occurred, according to the Bible

MERNEPTAH STELE

• duration of Israelites' bondage in Egypt

CANAAN

• Egypt's Nile Delta area where the Israelites settled after Joseph's time

IPUWER PAPYRUS

• a conclusion based on the lack of contrary evidence

GOSHEN

• possibly an Egyptian account of the ten plagues

LESSON 3

THE ISRAELITE CONQUEST

After the Israelites fled Egypt, God commanded them to settle in the "Promised Land." But in order to do so, they first had to conquer the Canaanite towns and cities, which included Jericho, Ai, and Hazor. The biblical texts document this fiery conquest at length, including a strange and miraculous story of the fall of Jericho.

Small details mentioned in these ancient writings can now be scrutinized in light of archaeological finds. Did Joshua really fight the battle of Jericho? Did the walls come tumbling down? If so, when? Let's allow the evidence to lead us to the most logical conclusion.

QUOTE UNQUOTE

What did Dr. Meyer say? Fill in the blanks as you watch his presentation..

1. From an archaeologist's point-of-view, there's nothing better than a good _____ _____.

2. Part of the reason that God condemns the Canaanites to this destruction is their idolatry, their _____ _____.

3. Biblical minimalists claim that any destruction evidence you find in these sites is from a series of indigenous _____ _____.

4. There's really not much doubt about the site for _____.

5. One way of dating an area is to look for distinctive styles of _____ that were known to characterize a particular era.

6. For some reason, the Egyptians really thought that _____ _____ were cool. . . . Whatever floats your boat, I guess.

7. In the Jericho burial grounds, you have inscriptions mentioning _____ that were not even alive yet in 1550 B.C.

8. [When] the walls fell outward, they formed a natural _____ that allowed Joshua's soldiers to go right in.

9. When the Bible makes _____ _____ claims, it invites _____ _____ testing.

10. What was one of the things that God commanded the Israelites to do as they entered these pagan cities? _____ _____ _____.

WHAT'S THE BIG IDEA?

THE WALLS CAME TUMBLIN' DOWN (AND WE FOUND THEM)

THE BIBLE'S ACCOUNT of the Israelite battle against Jericho is backed up by impressive archaeological evidence.

WHAT'S THE BIG IDEA?

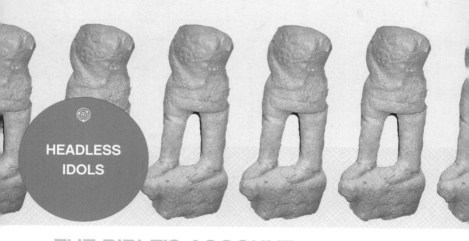

HEADLESS IDOLS

THE BIBLE'S ACCOUNT of the conquest of Hazor is also backed up by impressive archaeological evidence.

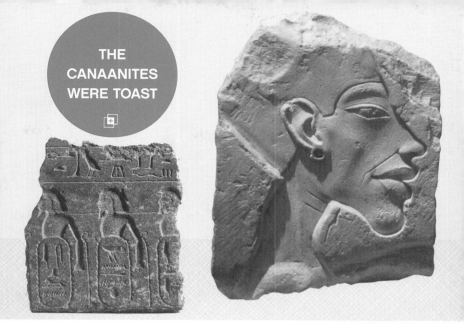

THE CANAANITES WERE TOAST

UNEARTHED EVIDENCE from key Canaanite cities and extra-biblical references to the presence of the Israelites confirm the main elements of the scriptural account of the conquest.

Do you get the feeling the Lord doesn't just want us to hand us Canaan . . .

But that He is really angry with the Canaanites?

Sacrificing innocent children to these phony gods might have something to do with it!

Discuss as a group what you would say if your teacher or professor asked the following question in class:

What specific evidence makes you think the Israelites conquered Jericho in the time and manner that the Bible describes?

You can refer to your notes, if you took any during Dr. Meyer's lecture. Describe each document, artifact, or other archaeological finding and how it relates to the Bible's account. Support or add to one another's responses so that the group can come up with a long list of evidence. Perhaps you'd like to role-play the dialogue, taking turns to represent the skeptical professor (or even Kathleen Kenyon herself).

Facts about Jericho (at the time of Joshua)

- A city with an ancient past (7000–8000 B.C.), often considered the oldest city in the world, repeatedly destroyed and rebuilt
- Important city, though only about 9–10 acres in size
- Situated on major trade routes
- Wedged into narrow fertile plain between the Jordan River and the mountains
- Home to several thousand people
- Fed by a perennial spring inside the city walls, yielding 1,000 gallons an hour
- A wonderful tropical oasis surrounded by date palms
- Strong fortress, with a very high set of walls (only one small section of the brick wall still stands today, suggestive of Rahab's house)
- So evil and steeped in idol worship that God wanted every living being—except for Rahab and her household—to be destroyed

"Have all the people give a loud shout; then the wall of the city will collapse and the people will go up, every man straight in."

—Joshua 6:5, NIV

"After the city walls fell, how did the Israelites surmount the four- to five-meter (12–15 foot) high retaining wall at the base of the tell? Excavations have shown that the bricks from the collapsed walls formed a ramp against the retaining wall so that the Israelites could merely climb up over the top."

—Archaeologist Bryant Wood

WHAT IS WHAT?

Draw a line from each term in the first column to its definition in the second column.

FIRE
• archaeologist who claimed that Jericho was destroyed much earlier than the Bible says

JERICHO
• city conquered by the Israelites on their second try

LATE BRONZE AGE I
• promising site for the ancient city of Ai

HAZOR
• type of pottery imported from Cyprus and used by the wealthy in 15th century B.C.

SCARAB
• there was a conquest, but it happened in the late 13th century B.C.

KENYON
• period of Middle Eastern history (roughly 1550–1400 B.C.) when Joshua entered the Promised Land

KHIRBET EL-MAQATIR
• last and largest city that the Israelites destroyed by fire

AI
• an archaeologist's best friend

EARLIER CONSENSUS VIEW
• first city that the Israelites conquered after crossing the Jordan

CYPRIOT
• large dung beetle regarded as sacred in ancient Egypt

LESSON 4

THE UNITED KINGDOM OF DAVID AND SOLOMON

The Old Testament reads like an epic—one grand story after another that portrays the might, sovereignty, grace, and salvation of the one true God who revealed Himself in the life of Israel. After establishing His people in the land of Canaan, God appointed His servant David to the throne. David was more than just a warrior-poet turned king; he was God's instrument in delivering the Israelites from oppression, defending the defenseless, crushing the wicked, and establishing a royal line through which the Messiah would eventually come. King David built a palace in the great city of Jerusalem. His son Solomon vastly expanded the kingdom and established the temple as the earthly throne of God.

However, this story too has been much maligned by the biblical minimalists, claiming that David either never existed or was simply a small tribal leader with little or no political power. We see once again that if one can discount the historicity of the Bible, its theological implications and message can also be dismissed. But if these stories prove to be true, then the message and meaning of the accounts must be taken seriously as well.

QUOTE UNQUOTE

What did Dr. Meyer say? Fill in the blanks as you watch his presentation..

1. As you get closer and closer to modern times, there's _____ corroborating evidence, _____ specificity in the evidence.

2. We think of David as the _____ figure in a child's story, . . . yet he's also a real figure in history.

3. Every single part of _____ history has been challenged by skeptics.

4. The minimalists insist that in 10th century B.C. Judah, there's little evidence of any permanent _____, no urban centers, no capital, no temple, and no big building projects.

5. Archaeology has provided some very compelling evidence for the reality of _____ as an urban center.

6. From 1230 B.C. right up to the beginning of the Davidic monarchy, we see the number of small villages in the central hill country go up from 29 to _____.

7. It's the largest Iron Age structure in Israel, and most archaeologists . . . think this is clearly the _____ ___ _____.

8. With almost every discovery in archaeology, there are _____.

9. _____ embarked on big building projects in key cities—Hazor, Megiddo, and Gezer.

10. _____ _____ is perhaps the most hotly contested piece of land on the entire planet.

WHAT'S THE BIG IDEA?

GOD'S METROPOLIS

Shekhna (Tel Leilan)
Haran
Alalakh
Nuzi
Mari
Babylon

Mediterranean Sea

Laish

Shechem
Salem
Hebron
— Sodom (Bab ed-Dhra)
Gomorrah (Numeira)

Ur

EGYPT

Persian Gulf

ARCHAEOLOGY HAS PROVED that Jerusalem was a large, important, and fortified city in the 10th century B.C.

STUPENDOUS STONES

ARCHAEOLOGY HAS UNEARTHED evidence
of David's and Solomon's building projects.

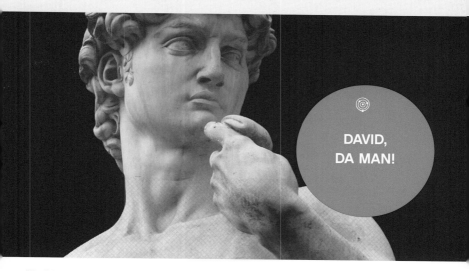

DAVID, DA MAN!

DAVID IS A REAL FIGURE IN HISTORY for whom
there is a great deal of extra-biblical evidence. The unbroken line of Davidic kings (the "House of David") lasted more than 400 years.

Discuss as a group what you would say if your teacher or professor asked the following question in class:

What proof is there that David was a real historical figure?

You can refer to your notes, if you took any during Dr. Meyer's lecture. Describe each document, artifact, or other archaeological finding and how it relates to the Bible's account. Support or add to one another's responses so that the group can come up with a long list of evidence. Perhaps you'd like to role-play the dialogue, taking turns to represent the minimalist professor or skeptical archaeologist.

Interview with an Archaeologist

NOVA: How important to your work is the text of the Bible?

Eilat Mazar: The Bible is the historical source, so important, so fantastically written. The question is, how much of the reality that the Bible describes can we archaeologists reveal? Sometimes you find something like the bulla with the name of a minister that appears in the Bible. This happens once in a while. More often you find structures that surely were constructed in ancient times, and the stones, the remains, speak. We need to listen to what they say.

"It seems to me that Jerusalem at the time of King David and King Solomon was very much like the Bible describes. It was monumental; the constructions were massive. They used the Phoenicians, with their capability and skill, to build the largest structures ever built in Jerusalem: the temple, the two palaces—King David's and later the palace of King Solomon—and the wall of Jerusalem around these structures."

—Eilat Mazar, who says she has found David's palace

Who Was David?

- second king of Israel
- a forgiven adulterer and murderer
- a man chosen by God (see 1 Samuel 13:14)
- author of most of the Bible's "songbook," the Psalms
- ancestor of Jesus Christ, the "son of David"

WHAT IS WHAT?

Draw a line from each term in the first column to its definition in the second column.

FINKELSTEIN

HOUSE OF DAVID

STEP STONE STRUCTURE

TEL DAN STELE

MESHA STELE

HADABIYAT-DAWIT

KURKH STELE

1010 B.C.

EILAT MAZAR

ELAH

- 9th-century B.C. basalt slab that mentions the "House of David"

- recent discoverer of David's palace

- approximate start of David's reign

- Israeli archaeologist and biblical minimalist at Tel Aviv University

- "the heights of David"

- valley where archaeologists found a gated fortress and a pottery shard mentioning a king

- 12-story-high wall discovered at Jerusalem by Kathleen Kenyon

- Assyrian monolith that mentions King Ahab

- the 400-year line of kings begun by David

- stone on which the king of Moab claims to have wiped out Israel

LESSON 5

HISTORICITY OF THE OLD TESTAMENT: A TALE OF TWO CONQUESTS

The Davidic monarchy lasted more than four hundred years and saw God's people become major players in the history of the Middle East. But the Bible describes their unfaithfulness to the Lord, which led to their punishment when both the northern kingdom of Israel and the southern kingdom of Judah were attacked by the Assyrian Empire.

This lesson examines the archaeological record of Sennacherib's assault on Judah. We learn how the evidence backs up the Bible's account of the defense of Jerusalem. God intervened in that siege when Judah's king, Hezekiah, turned to Him for help. So again, we have actual historical events and a God who intervenes in human affairs. Let's look at the evidence for this amazing story.

QUOTE UNQUOTE

What did Dr. Meyer say? Fill in the blanks as you watch his presentation..

1. The Davidic monarchy stretched from about the year 1000 B.C. until it finally ended with the destruction of Jerusalem in 587 B.C. by the _____.

2. In about 701 B.C., following the conquest of Israel, the Assyrians moved on to attack the kingdom of _____.

3. _____ is one big dude. This is not an empire you want to be messing with.

4. We found the seal, a little signet ring, bearing his name and the name of one of his officials, Abdi, servant of _____.

5. As you're approaching Jerusalem, you have to come through the mountain pass that goes through _____ and Lachish.

6. Excavations of _____ have uncovered about 1,500 skulls and hundreds of Assyrian arrowheads.

7. An angel of the Lord came in the middle of the night and caused _____ Assyrians to die.

8. There was no conquest of _____ despite the fact that the most powerful empire in the world was now laying siege to this city.

9. When we get to this period at the end of the Davidic monarchy, guess what happens? The _____ say almost nothing.

10. There are ____ significant challenges to the historicity of these narratives.

.

WHAT'S THE BIG IDEA?

ASSYRIA'S
THREAT

ARCHAEOLOGY HAS YIELDED ample proof that
Assyria attacked Israel and Judah exactly as the Bible records.

WHAT'S THE BIG IDEA?

185,000 TO 0—
GAME OVER

EXTRA-BIBLICAL EVIDENCE SHOWS

that Jerusalem was indeed protected from Sennacherib's army as a result of King Hezekiah's trust in the Lord, just as the Bible says.

Sennacherib, your highness, our entire army dropped dead overnight!

All 185,000? Bummer!

Hmmm, maybe all Gods are *not* the same!

PROFESSOR SAYS, YOU SAY

What specific things about the Assyrian assault on Judah show agreement between the biblical record and the archaeological or documentary evidence?

You can refer to your notes, if you took any during Dr. Meyer's lecture. For each piece of evidence, tell the group what the document or artifact is called and what it proves. (If possible, include where it was discovered.) Support or add to one another's responses so that the group can come up with a long list of evidence. Perhaps you'd like to role-play the dialogue, taking turns to represent the skeptical professor.

Interesting Facts

- *Jewish sources claim that the archangel Gabriel is the one who destroyed Assyria's 185,000 troops.*

- *Egyptians attributed Sennacherib's defeat at Jerusalem to field mice that ate the Assyrians' bowstrings.*

- *Hezekiah hated idolatry so much that he even destroyed Moses' famous bronze serpent after people began to worship it (2 Kings 18:4).*

- *Sennacherib was murdered while worshiping Nisroch, an eagle-headed idol that some believe was a demon.*

WHAT IS WHAT?

Draw a line from each term in the first column to its definition in the second column.

JUDAH

• number of fenced Judean cities that Sennacherib conquered

30 TALENTS OF GOLD

• Judean city that Sennacherib brags about destroying

HOSHEA

• Assyrian king assassinated by his own sons

CONSPICUOUS SILENCE

• where Assyrian arrowheads have been discovered

AZEKAH

• southern kingdom with Jerusalem as capital

SENNACHERIB

• last king of Israel (the northern kingdom)

46

• Jerusalem's source of water while under attack

HEZEKIAH

• Sennacherib's failure to mention conquering Jerusalem

LACHISH

• king of Judea who trusted God

HEZEKIAH'S TUNNEL

• part of Hezekiah's tribute to Sennacherib

LESSON 6

THE BABYLONIAN CONQUEST OF JUDAH

The Christian worldview attests not only to the existence of God, but also to His sovereignty over history. It is in fact His story, not ours. He started the story with His creative work, He continues to act providentially within history, and one day He will bring the story to its ultimate climax through His return. History is simply the outworking of the divine plan to bring all of creation back under His rule and establish His kingdom on earth as it is in heaven.

This particular lesson describes the destruction of Jerusalem by the Babylonians, thereby ending the Davidic monarchy. Due to Israel's rebellion against Him, God handed them over to their enemies to be taken into exile. Once again, through historical events we can see the love, patience, mercy, and judgment of the creator God on and for His people.

These stories aren't myths; they weave together a delicate and beautiful tapestry of events that not only demonstrate God's existence but also show His unfailing love for His people and His control over history.

QUOTE UNQUOTE

What did Dr. Meyer say? Fill in the blanks as you watch his presentation.

1. When we get to this account of the destruction of Jerusalem in 605 B.C., the _____ are nowhere to be found.

2. You find the passion of God . . . spoken through _____.

3. At the battle of _____, Nebuchadnezzar defeats Necho.

4. The prophet Jeremiah warned _____ that God had decided to put the Judahites under the control of Nebuchadnezzar.

5. _____ and _____ are always the last two cities to fall.

6. I found I could not stay away from Jerusalem and the _____ _____.

7. In Jeremiah 36 you've got _____ biblical figures corroborated by extra-biblical findings.

8. We have no right to expect this level of _____ for any event that long ago.

9. We've seen that in _____, _____ _____ , and in the great movements of history, the biblical record is accurate.

WHAT'S THE BIG IDEA?

BAD DUDES FROM BABYLON

THE BIBLICAL ACCOUNT of the Babylonian conquest of Judah contains many details supported by external evidence, making these events some of the most well-attested in history.

King Nebuchadnezzar, these chronicles speak well of your victories for Babylon . . .

But will future generations believe your testimony?

Certainly, because I'll have extra-chronicle corraboration!

Meaning what, sir?

The Hebrew scriptures, of course. That prophet Jeremiah will back up my story.

NOT JUST
"BIBLE STORIES"

WE TELL OURSELVES THAT WE believe the Bible's historical accounts, but when we see actual proof that these events happened, it finally sinks in that all of this is for real—the events and the God who acted in them.

So, my young friends of Jeremiah, that concludes our look at evidence that Abraham really lived.

Gives me the shivers. I often thought of Abraham as just a Bible story.

Be careful. How would you feel if someday you were considered just a Bible story?

Discuss as a group what you would say if your teacher or professor asked the following question in class:

What possible evidence is there to prove that the biblical record is true concerning Nebuchadnezzar's conquest over Judah?

You can refer to your notes, if you took any during Dr. Meyer's lecture. For each piece of evidence, tell the group what the document or artifact is called and what it proves. (If possible, include where it was discovered.) Support or add to one another's responses so that the group can come up with a long list of evidence. Perhaps you'd like to role-play the dialogue, taking turns to represent the skeptical professor.

Bullae for Us

What happens to clay when it's exposed to fire? It becomes hardened. And that explains why the little blobs of clay that citizens of ancient Israel used to seal documents—stamping the clay with their signet ring—have brought us impressive proof of the Bible's reliability.

The fires that destroyed Jerusalem (2 Kings 25:9) under the assault of the Babylonian army also helped preserve these "bullae" for our benefit. So now we know that Jeremiah's friend and scribe, Baruch son of Neriah (Jeremiah 36:4), along with several other key officials mentioned in Jeremiah's account of events, really lived.

It's a good thing they didn't use wax seals in those days. Or, for that matter, e-mail.

WHAT IS WHAT?

Draw a line from each term in the first column to its definition in the second column.

ZEDEKIAH

JEHOIACHIN

OSTRACON

BABYLON

NECHO

NEBUCHADNEZZAR

CYRUS

JEHOIAKIM

587 B.C.

VASSAL

- ancient city-state located just south of modern Baghdad

- first king of Judah to rebel against Nebuchadnezzar

- a person or country in a subordinate position to another

- Persian king who conquered Babylon

- son of Jehoiakim

- Egyptian pharaoh defeated at Battle of Carchemish

- shard of pottery with writing on it

- Babylonian destruction of Jerusalem

- Babylonian king who conquered Judah

- last king of Judah before the destruction

LESSON 7

CANONS OF HISTORICITY: THE NEW TESTAMENT

The last two hundred years of biblical scholarship have produced a hostile and critical view of the New Testament writings. Critics claim transmission errors, dating problems, authorship concerns, and a lack of extra-biblical sources verifying what really happened.

Recent archaeological finds, however, have unearthed mounds of evidence that are slowly bringing the age of skepticism to its end. The apostle Paul encouraged the believer to "test everything" (1Thessalonians 5:21, NIV) to determine truth. That is exactly what we are doing in this series. By looking at the evidence, studying the recent findings, and corroborating the stories, we realize there really is no good reason to doubt the accuracy of the New Testament.

QUOTE UNQUOTE

What did Dr. Meyer say? Fill in the blanks as you watch his presentation.

1. It's not hard to find critics of the reliability of the _____ _____.

2. Skepticism about the New Testament started right back at the end of the _____ century.

3. Some of those critical ideas have made their way into popular novels and books like _____ ___ _____ _____.

4. The New Testament is one of the most _____ books or series of books of antiquity.

5. There are ways of analyzing whether or not the documents we currently possess have been reliably _____.

6. A document that's written _____ to the time of the events it describes is going to have more historical value.

7. It's clear that _____ is setting forth a very systematic historical description of the life of Jesus of Nazareth.

8. The _____ _____ has been preserved in more ancient manuscripts than any other document from antiquity.

9. The New Testament clearly has documents within it, like the Gospels, that display a _____ genre or style of writing.

10. We have good reason to be confident that the New Testament has come down to us in much the same form as its original _____.

WHAT'S THE BIG IDEA?

WHO, WHAT, WHEN, WHERE, WHY

OUR CONFIDENCE in the New Testament's historical reliability is based in part on the evidence that most of it was written to document actual events.

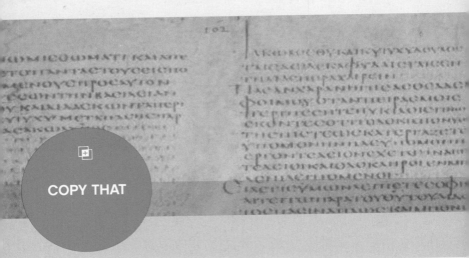

COPY THAT

OUR CONFIDENCE in the New Testament's historical accuracy is based also on the evidence that the original documents were reliably transmitted to us over the centuries.

We've already made 500 identical copies of this Gospel!

Brother Xero, please keep writing.

I wish we had a machine where we could pop in the original and get lots of copies.

Bless you, brother, you have a wild imagination!

Discuss as a group what you would say if your teacher or professor asked the following questions in class:

Why is it important to you that the New Testament be historically accurate?

Can't you still have your religion without that?

The teachings of Jesus are very good, so can't you just follow those teachings whether Jesus was a real person or not?

You can refer to your notes, if you took any during Dr. Meyer's lecture. For each piece of evidence, tell the group what the document or artifact is called and what it proves. (If possible, include where it was discovered.) Support or add to one another's responses so that the group can come up with a long list of evidence. Perhaps you'd like to role-play the dialogue, taking turns to represent the skeptical professor.

History and Theology Intertwined

"It is, indeed, difficult to restrict a discussion of the New Testament writings to the purely historical plane; theology insists on breaking in. But that is as it should be; history and theology are inextricably intertwined in the gospel of our salvation, which owes its eternal and universal validity to certain events which happened in Palestine when Tiberius ruled the Roman Empire."

—F. F. Bruce,
The New Testament Documents:
Are They Reliable?

WHAT IS WHAT?

Draw a line from each term in the first column to its definition in the second column.

TRANSMISSION	• 5th-century manuscript of the Greek Bible
BULTMANN	• confirming or supporting with additional evidence
THEOPHILUS	• expert in the study of ancient manuscripts
CODEX ALEXANDRINUS	• purporting to give a factual report; not fiction
JESUS SEMINAR	• to accurately pass something on to the next generation
MAGDALEN PAPYRUS	• fragments of the Greek Bible dating as far back as A.D. 150
PALEOGRAPHER	• German theologian who called for "demythologizing" the New Testament
CHESTER BEATTY PAPYRI	• group of scholars who say the "historical Jesus" was just a man with a message, not God Himself
DOCUMENTARY STYLE	• ancient scrap of the book of Matthew studied by Peter Thiede
CORROBORATION	• man to whom Luke dedicated both the Gospel of Luke and Acts of the Apostles

LESSON 8

EARLY COMPOSITION OF LUKE AND ACTS

The Gospel of Luke is the prequel to the book of Acts, and Luke, a fellow worker with Paul, wrote both. From the outset, Luke informs his reader that he is writing history. In fact, Luke states that he is simply writing down eyewitness accounts, and writing very close to the date when these events took place. Luke is not writing propaganda, fiction, or myth. And yet scholars are troubled by the message of both books because in Luke's historical record, he presents Jesus as both Messiah and Lord, proclaiming the historical truth of Jesus' bodily resurrection.

As you move into academia and culture, you will find professors and peers who attack Scripture based not so much on historical facts but on their presuppositions or worldview. Understanding why someone believes what he believes is half the battle. Take the time to understand the worldviews that drive so many to reject the historicity and claims of Scripture; in so doing, you may earn enough credibility to explain the what and why of your own beliefs.

QUOTE UNQUOTE

What did Dr. Meyer say? Fill in the blanks as you watch his presentation.

1. _____, _____, and _____ have a very straightforward documentary style.

2. In all three of the synoptics, Jesus is recorded as having predicted . . . the _____ ___ _____.

3. If you hold a naturalistic worldview, is it possible to tell what's going to happen before it happens? No, that's called _____.

4. If we are able to date the book of Acts, what will we also get to know about the book of Luke? It's going to be _____.

5. Luke is a _____ historian because he gets all those nitty-gritty details absolutely right.

6. The tone toward the Romans throughout the book of Acts is very _____.

7. There's no mention [in the book of Acts] of the death of _____, _____, or _____.

8. New Testament scholars think that _____, the shortest Gospel, is a source for Luke.

9. There are good reasons to believe that Luke and Acts and Mark were written _____ to the time of the events they record.

WHAT'S THE BIG IDEA?

YOU HAD TO BE THERE

OUR CONFIDENCE in the New Testament's historical reliability is based in part on the evidence that it was composed soon after the events it describes.

Discuss as a group what you would say if your teacher or professor asked the following questions in class:

How can you possibly know that the book called the "Acts of the Apostles" is historically accurate?

Specifically, that it was written close to the time of the events it claims to recount?

You can refer to your notes, if you took any during Dr. Meyer's lecture. For each piece of evidence, tell the group what the document or artifact is called and what it proves. (If possible, include where it was discovered.) Support or add to one another's responses so that the group can come up with a long list of evidence. Perhaps you'd like to role-play the dialogue, taking turns to represent the skeptical professor.

Copious Copies

"In comparison with the remaining manuscripts of any other ancient Greek or Latin literature, the New Testament suffers from an embarrassment of riches. It is almost incomprehensible to think about the disparity. When it comes to quantity of copies, the New Testament has no peer. More than 5,700 Greek New Testament manuscripts are still in existence, ranging in date from the early second century to the sixteenth century."

— *Dr. Daniel B. Wallace in ESV Study Bible*

Chief of the Island

It was a good day for the people of Malta when the ship carrying the apostle Paul ran aground on the island (Acts 27:41). Through Paul, the Lord healed the father of Publius, the "chief man of the island" (28:7), as well as many others.

Publius was later appointed the first bishop of Malta, and he is said to have been martyred by the Romans around A.D. 125. Malta eventually became regarded as one of the first Christian nations in the world. Catholicism is still the official and dominant religion of that country.

WHAT IS WHAT?

Draw a line from each term in the first column to its definition in the second column.

LYSANIAS
• proconsul of Achaia

PROCONSUL
• a judge's raised platform in ancient Rome

JOHN A.T. ROBINSON
• Jewish historian

GALLIO
• Tetrarch of Abilene

YOU-HAD-TO-BE-THERE PRINCIPLE
• peaceable, neutral

SERGIUS PAULUS
• author of the "Acts of the Apostles"

JOSEPHUS
• governor of a senatorial province in ancient Rome

IRENIC
• proconsul of Cyprus

JUDGMENT SEAT
• author of Honest to God

LUKE
• the idea that you could know specific details only if you had witnessed an event or obtained information from an eyewitness

LESSON 9

EXTERNAL CORROBORATION

The people and places of the New Testament have been externally corroborated by archaeology and primary source material, such as the writings of the historian Flavius Josephus. Whether studying the major political figures of the day like Herod the Great or average people like Erastus, we know these individuals lived during the time of Jesus, providing further evidence for the historical truth of Scripture.

As the evidence continues to build, it is becoming harder and harder to doubt the historicity of the New Testament. Stories, places, individuals, and events continue to be verified, bolstering our confidence in the reliability of the early Christian writings.

QUOTE UNQUOTE

What did Dr. Meyer say? Fill in the blanks as you watch his presentation.

1. The Gospels and other parts of the New Testament clearly have a _____ style.

2. It's actually uncanny how accurate the book of _____ is.

3. As archaeologists have excavated in the area around Cana . . . they have found a preponderance of _____ waterpots.

4. Today there is in Samaria a well that is, by tradition, thought to be _____ well.

5. The pool [of Bethesda] has certainly been discovered; so have those distinctive five covered _____.

6. If you go under the ruins of that 4th-century synagogue [in Capernaum], guess what's been discovered? A 1st-century _____.

7. Not all tombs [in Bethany] were _____ _____.

8. Herod was a really big builder, and the _____ _____ was expanded dramatically when he was in power.

9. Historians tend to regard _____ _____ of extreme significance.

10. Only _____ or _____ people had their bones placed in ossuaries.

WHAT'S THE BIG IDEA?

PLACES AND
PLAYERS

SIGNIFICANT CORROBORATION between
external evidence and the people and places of the New Testament gives
us confidence in the Bible's historical reliability.

Discuss as a group what you would say if your teacher or professor asked the following questions in class:

How can you say that the Gospel of John is a historical document?

What evidence is there that the places it mentions once existed?

You can refer to your notes, if you took any during Dr. Meyer's lecture. For each piece of evidence, tell the group what the document or artifact is called and what it proves. (If possible, include where it was discovered.) Support or add to one another's responses so that the group can come up with a long list of evidence. Perhaps you'd like to role-play the dialogue, taking turns to represent the skeptical professor.

Herod's Happy Place?

In September 2010, even more evidence of Herod the Great and his opulent lifestyle was unearthed at the Herodium, a vast country club/fortress that Herod built on a hill just south of Jerusalem. Herod's tomb was discovered here in 2007. A 400-seat amphitheater, built around 15 B.C., was excavated in 2008. Most recently, archaeologists have revealed Herod's private theater box, elaborately decorated with Roman wall paintings and plaster moldings. Imagine the ruler entertaining his friends in style while pondering his order to kill all male infants in Bethlehem (Matthew 2:16), or his execution of a wife, former mother-in-law, and three sons.

WHAT IS WHAT?

Draw a line from each term in the first column to its definition in the second column.

ERASTUS

• place where Jesus healed a lifelong invalid

CAPERNAUM

• soil residue that collects on an artifact over time

ASSUMPTION OF MOSES

• arched recess used as a burial place

POOL OF BETHESDA

• public employee at Corinth

POOL OF SILOAM

• document attesting to the existence of Herod

PATINA

• Samaritan woman's source of drinking water

ATTEST

• bone box

ARCOSOLIUM

• village on north shore of Sea of Galilee

JACOB'S WELL

• place where Jesus healed a blind man

OSSUARY

• serve as clear evidence

Jesus is the most important person in human history—assuming that He really lived, and that He died and rose again according to the scriptural accounts. In this final lesson of TrueU's "Is the Bible Reliable?" Dr. Meyer culminates his defense of Scripture by studying the trial of Jesus. Specifically, he examines extra-biblical sources that attest to the historicity of several individuals who played a key role in the events of that momentous week.

In conclusion, go forth with courage and strength, knowing that what you believe really is real, that it rests on solid historical facts and can be trusted with your very life.

QUOTE UNQUOTE

What did Dr. Meyer say? Fill in the blanks as you watch his presentation.

1. One-_____ of the Gospels are devoted to an account of the trial of Jesus and His death by crucifixion.

2. We see in Luke 23 that Herod _____ is very glad to see Jesus.

3. _____ happens to have authored two first-person narratives in which he identifies himself as the author.

4. Often we have the sense that biblical history is really a bunch of _____ _____ .

5. _____ was the Jewish high priest from A.D. 18 to 36, and he organized the plot to kill Jesus.

6. We really have no reason to doubt the _____ of Jesus of Nazareth.

7. Recently a version of _____ has been discovered that did not pass through Christian hands.

8. We saw that Tacitus, the Roman historian, . . . attested to Pontius Pilate, but that passage also mentions not Christ but "_____."

9. You get the feeling . . . that the basic facts of the life of Jesus of Nazareth were _____ _____.

10. One of the things that's most exciting about the faith is that truth stands up to _____.

WHAT'S THE BIG IDEA?

THE EVENT OF ALL TIME

WE KNOW THAT THE TRIAL and death of Jesus actually happened because five of the key people involved—especially Jesus Himself—have been independently attested by ample documentary and inscriptional evidence.

Discuss as a group what you would say if your teacher or professor asked the following questions in class:

Some of the teachings in the Gospels are admirable. But how do you know Jesus was a real person?

What sources besides the Bible are you relying on?

You can refer to your notes, if you took any during Dr. Meyer's lecture. For each piece of evidence, tell the group what the document or artifact is called and what it proves. (If possible, include where it was discovered.) Support or add to one another's responses so that the group can come up with a long list of evidence. Perhaps you'd like to role-play the dialogue, taking turns to represent the skeptical professor.

Peter's Pad— The Ultimate House Church

Near the ancient synagogue in Capernaum, archaeologists have found a first-century house that appears to have been transformed into a house church only a few years after Jesus' death and resurrection. Architectural changes suggest that the building was used for larger meetings, while numerous inscriptions include the name of Jesus and various crosses and other symbols. Today, a modern church building rests on the site, with a glass floor that allows people to look down upon the house once occupied by Peter and perhaps Jesus Himself.

LESSON 10

THE
TRIAL
OF JESUS